The Hydroponic garden secrets

A BEGINNERS HYDROPONIC GUIDE TO BUILD THE BEST GROWING SYSTEM AND AN INEXPENSIVE GARDEN. HOW TO GROW FRUITS, VEGETABLES, AND PLANTS

AT YOUR HOME

TYLER BRAY

TABLE OF CONTENTS

Introduction

Water is the essential ingredient of all life, and it has an especially vital role in the life of plants. Water provides the transport of nutrients and energy (salts and sugars) to the cells within a plant. Unfortunately, the soil and environment that plants generally grow in are far from perfect. Therefore, the goal with hydroponics is to try to replicate what occurs in a perfectly natural and optimal growing setting. This is achieved by consistently enriching the water with nutrients, and then making these available for absorption by our plants. We refer to this water as a balanced 'nutrient solution.'

The nutrient solution that you will supply is generally provided through a human-made embedded system. This gives rise to the benefit of avoiding the evaporation that occurs in soil. In other words, we are ensuring that this nutrient-rich water is always available to our plants when they require it. Whether you know it or not, you have likely already practiced simple hydroponics by putting flowers in a vase and adding a ready-made nutrient solution.

Hydroponics is consistently growing in popularity in the modern world, from backyard ventures to hydroponic applications on space stations! Hydroponics will play a key role in being able to provide nutrition as humans continue to explore the possibility of living on other planets. On a more fundamental level, hydroponics offers an affordable means of producing food for low-income areas of the world and the popularity of growing hydroponically as a hobby has gained a fair deal of popularity over recent decades.

A great way to describe hydroponic gardening is to say that it is a soil-free type of gardening. Great leaps in technology have allowed plants to grow without soil. However, this unique way of planting that is rapidly becoming popular has been around for decades.

This is the Hanging Gardens of Babylon. These early forms of hydroponic gardening were placed on top of ziggurats, which were watered through dividing channels, and supplied with water from the Euphrates River.

Ancient Mexico also had its version of hydroponic gardening. Floating gardens, or chinampas, are gardens with plants grown in a lake in ancient Mexico.

However, the ultimate origin of hydroponic gardening occurs in nature itself. No human interference or structures took place in this naturally produced hydroponic garden.

For example, orchids are the most significant examples of hydroponic gardening. They have aerial roots that innately do not need soil to thrive.

Hydroponics is seen as the next step in the evolution of agriculture by many experts as it has revolutionized the ability to grow plants and crops. It is most often used in greenhouses to experiment with and grow different varieties of plants. Hydroponics is revolutionary because it eliminates the need for what was considered a major element for growing plants and crops, namely soil.

There are three components that plants require to grow correctly i.e., water, air (oxygen and carbon dioxide), and soil.

The principle behind hydroponics is that soil provides the mineral nutrients required by plants as well as the solid medium in which they "anchor" their roots. However, it has been discovered that plants can absorb the minerals and nutrients required for proper growth from liquid medium and solutions.

Hydroponics is becoming a widely accepted technique for growing healthy and nutritious vegetables, fruits, and flowers both indoor and outdoor. It also provides us the most robust crops containing the highest number of vitamins, minerals, and nutrients and that too in a minimum space. Today, many farmers worldwide are using hydroponics for producing fruits, vegetables, and flowers because of the technique's ability to produce rich nutrients and minerals and high yields. Many farmers are claiming that their production capacity has increased many-fold after using hydroponics.

Today, we are becoming more prone to diseases, and we are putting a substantial amount of chemicals and pesticides inside our body using traditional farming products. These agricultural products have such a large amount of chemicals that some physicians have proscribed their use in some patients suffering from diabetes, high blood pressure, and allergies. Now, many people are diverting to natural forms of cultivation such as organic farming and hydroponics. If you have a small family and you think that traditional food products are harming your health, then hydroponics is the best way to provide a regular source of fruits and vegetables rich in nutrients, vitamins, and minerals. You can quickly grow them on your property with very little space and minimum investment. Hydroponics is also a great way for some commercial farmers and nursery owners to increase their profit and sales.

A simple hydroponic system typically contains the following essential elements:

Nutrient solution: A solution of water, essential nutrients, and oxygen supply that directly comes in contact with the roots of your hydroponic plants.

Plant holding material: This comprises a holding cup; containing holes to supply essential nutrients, and a base in which these cups should be placed.

Substrates: In hydroponics, soil is not used, therefore there must be a substrate to hold the plant firmly for growth. Some commonly used substrates are sand, rice husk, coconut fiber, and volcanic stones.

Dissolved oxygen supply: Our plant needs a direct oxygen supply for proper growth, and we provide it with a simple mechanism.

A hydroponic garden is not designed for large-scale farming activities, so your choice of crops to have on your garden matters. Generally, when it comes to vegetables, consider the following principles:

- Choose crops that do not occupy a vast area per plant.

- Give preference to fast-growing crops, especially those that take about 3 to 4 months or less to start yielding.

- If you are planting crops that take longer to mature, they should be those that continue to give yields over a long period of time.

- Consider crops that do not have a wide canopy so that you can have variety in your garden. A canopy will deny other plants much-needed sunlight to grow well.

Chapter – 1
WHAT IS HYDROPONIC GARDENING

Across history, many various civilizations have utilized hydroponic growing technique. Through his book Hydroponic Food production, Howard M. Resh states that the hanging gardens of Babylon, the floating gardens of the Mexican Aztecs and those of the Chinese are manifestations of 'Hydroponic' society. This went on to claim the hieroglyphic records dated from Egypt several hundred years ago B.C. Describe the plant which grows in water. Since the area's environment was dry, yet rarely saw the weather, people claim that the ancient Babylonians used a chain pull tool to water the field plants.

With this method, water was taken from the river and carried up through the chain network and dropped to steps or landings in the greenhouse.

Accordingly, other records of Hydroponics in the ancient era were identified by the Aztecs of Mexico with floating farms around the island town of Tenochtitlan in the 10th and 11th centuries. Additionally, in his late 13th century literature the adventurer, Marco Polo, noted that he saw identical floating gardens during his trip to China.

Although hydroponics is an ancient way of growing plants, this revolutionary field of agriculture has made huge strides over the years.

Development of Hydroponics

The concept of hydroponics is nothing what you can say is fresh or new as Preceded earliest tillage methods on fields, and from time immemorial plants were produced in oceans and lakes.

It is important to remember that the history of today's hydroponics technique can be traced in the past to the middle of 15th century, once Leonardo da Vinci (Birth Date 1452), concluded:

It is common knowledge that plants for their development require mineral elements which they absorb through the water from soil. Hence, the plants cannot survive without water, irrespective to the fact that the soil possesses all the essential things that plants require.

Put in another way, water acts as a soul for plants, just like minerals perform the functions of the soul for soil. This means that unless we could pass the power of the core of soil (minerals) to the core of plants (water), then we will not require it (soil) to make the plants grow and reproduce.

He later advised to add fertilizer and irrigate the lands periodically in order to acquire a fit and dynamic plantation."

The Starting Years of Hydroponics

A review of history indicates that it was not before 1600 that there were documented scientific experiments which were done on plant nutrition and growth. The Belgian scientist, Jan Van Helmont, performed experiments and indicated that plants acquired materials from water. But he did not get to know that from the oxygen and carbon dioxide present in air is also essential for plants

Moreover, hydroponics, like we all know, it evolved gradually from the Middle Centuries before water culture has become a popular study technique throughout the Seventeenth century, afterwards published posthumously by the researcher Francis Bacon of a publication on this topic.

It was in 1699 that investigators establish that plants generally grew healthier in the less clean water than that in the distilled water. A researcher, John Woodward, began to study the growth of plants using water. Woodward discovered that plants grew best in water that has a large quantity of soil. Consequently, he concluded that such soil-derived compounds in the water contributed to plant production, rather than water itself.

Plethora of subsequent studies were carried out until 1804 when De Saussure suggested that plants were made of chemical elements obtained from water, air, and soil.

A French chemist, Boussignault, verified this proposal in 1851. The French experimented with growing plants without soil in an unsolvable artificial environment, including, quartz, sand, and charcoal. Boussignault the French chemist used chemical nutrients and water only for this experiment. He consequently discovered that plants require water and obtain hydrogen through it; plants' dry matter includes hydrogen with oxygen carbon and from the air; plants contain nitrogen and many other nutrients.

From 1860 to 1861 a conclusion was obtained of an extensive search for the necessary nutrient supply for plant production, when two German botanists, Julius von Sachs, and Wilhelm Knop, provided the first basic formula where plants could be developed for water-dissolved nutrient solutions. The finding of that formula contributed to the root of "nutriculture." This is called Water Culture in modern-day world. In the latter process, plant roots were fully submerged in solution of water containing nitrogen (N), phosphorus (P), potassium (K), magnesium (Mg), sulfur (S), and calcium (Ca). Such elements are often called the macro-elements

Surprisingly enough, however, the system of

plants developing in nutrient solution, water was used primarily as tests and utilized mainly in plant science laboratories.

Julius Sachs, a German botanist at the University of Würzburg, devoted his work in the 19th century to recognizing the basic elements plants need to thrive. Through analyzing variations between plants grown in soil and those grown in water, Sachs noticed that plants did not need to grow in soil but require only the nutrients obtained from micro-organisms that reside in soil. In 1860, Sachs published the method for growing plants in water, dubbed "nutrient solution," which laid the basis for modern hydroponic technology.

Furthermore, Researchers have expressed revived attention in plant growth and nutrient needs in the Nineteenth century. Nutrient solutions over the time were produced, but it was just in the 1920s when Professor from USA, WF Gericke (University of California), started to concentrate on agricultural plant growth utilizing dissolved nutrient solutions instead of soil. WF Gericke created the name 'hydroponics'.

It was in 1937 that Dr. W.E. Gericke explained how this process of growing plants could be used to harvest vast numbers of crops for agricultural use. Gericke and others showed that water's fluid dynamics modified the design of plant roots, allowing them to consume nutrients more quickly than plants growing in soil, helping them develop larger in a shorter period of time.

He began spreading the drill of plants growing in a water solution when he was at the U.C. Berkley.

Unfortunately, he came across to the doubt from the community and university. Even the colleagues of W.E. Gericke's rejected the idea of using the greenhouses (on-ground) for his research. He proved them incorrect by growing 20 plus foot tall plants of tomato in solutions filled with nutrients successfully.

However, The University again questioned its positive cultivation record, and asked 2 other students to examine its argument. Gericke's students published the study and announced their results in a 1938 agricultural journal, called "The Water Culture System for Growing Plants without Soil." Gericke's students acknowledged the practice of Hydroponics but concluded that crops grown by Hydroponics are no better than those grown on standard soils. Yet in contrast with the traditional practice they skipped much of the benefits of agricultural hydroponics. Since then, scientists have optimized the nutrient solution, a total of 13 macronutrients and micronutrients that are added to water for hydroponic farming.

At the moment, greenhouse farmers removed, or preserved, their greenhouse soil by applying vast amounts of agricultural fertilizers at regular intervals. Scientists have substituted natural soil structures with either ventilated nutrient solution or unnatural soil, which is called substrates, made of chemical inert masses, dampened with nutrient solutions to address this issue.

The Later Years of Hydroponics

While substantial development took place from 1920 and 1940 in changing the methods used by plant physiologists for wide-scale crop growth, hydroponics generally was not adopted because of the high expense of building growing beds made of concrete.

Throughout World War II, the U.S. army started utilizing hydroponics to generate foodstuff for troops deployed with in South Atlantic islands as well as Pacific islands, owing to the expensive shipping costs. Thus, the first well-known use of Hydroponic plant production was on Wake Island, an island with no soil in the Pacific Ocean, in the early 1940s. Pan American Airlines used this island as a refilling station. The shortage of soil has indicated that growing with the traditional method is not possible and airlifting of fresh vegetables was enormously costly. Hydroponics addressed the issues impressively thriving and delivered all the troops on this remote island with new vegetables. Hydroponic farming was also commonly used by the Army after World War II. The military of U.S cultivated a 22-ha plantation in Japan. (at Chofu)

In 1950s, hydroponics' soilless approach spread to a number of nations, including, Italy, Spain, England, France Sweden, Israel, and USSR.

Interestingly, when the war was over, the attentiveness in hydroponics flourished as hydroponic gravel culture was used for the production of various vegetables. These structures, though, had limitations and, ultimately, all were abandoned.

Plastic revolution and Hydroponics

Throughout the years of 1950s, the introduction of plastic sheets as wrapping material sparked a revived interest throughout hydroponics. Glass was substituted by plastic and permitted smaller, lower-cost systems for operations in controlled environment agriculture (CEA). Further, the tunnels and greenhouses made of plastic have been popular all around the globe, and the phenomenon continues today. The costlier concrete rising past beds were supplemented by plastic row coverings and troughs, while plastic tubing, cheaper filters, drip irrigation, and plastic basins were also added, among others.

Numerous strategies also emerged to support hydroponics, contributing to Wide-range expenditure in hydroponic systems.

Scientists and horticulturists also dealt with numerous hydroponic techniques during the last century. In addition, one of the possible uses of hydroponics that motivated research was growing food in the world's non-arable areas and areas with little or no soil. During World War II, Hydroponics was used to deliver fresh produce grown in locally developed hydroponic systems to troops posted on non-arable Pacific islands.

Chapter - 2
HYDROPONIC VS SOIL

Soil Gardening

Soil gardening, as you know, is more affordable because the equipment needed are just simple tools and types of machinery, nothing ambiguous. Plus, typically, you do not need to adjust so much about the soil as it does this itself, using its environment as a gage. Since plants will naturally grow on soil, it is only natural for the soil to be gentle on plants. Overall, soil gardening seems so much easier than hydroponics, what is not to love?

Well, those are only the good sides; would you be able to deal with the bad sides?

First off, it takes longer for plants to grow in the soil. You will also notice defects late because it takes longer for these defects to become visible. What this means is that the defects would have done so much damage before they are finally noticed, ultimately making the recovery of the plants difficult and longer. This could take its toll on your money and your time.

Then, at the beginning of your plant's growth in the soil, it will require all the attention and patience as it is still tender and quite vulnerable.

You also have to deal with preventing bugs from feasting on your plants. This is an almost impossible feat, and it is best to stick with hydroponics if you cannot deal with the bugs.

Hydroponic Gardening

In hydroponic gardening, you have total control over the nutrient supply provided to your plants. This will help minimize problems that usually develop from an inadequate nutrient supply in the soil.

You also skip so much growing time and get to harvest real quick because the nutrients come directly to your plants and your plants do not expend so much time and energy in search of nutrients, as is the case in soil gardening. They, therefore, spend most of the time and energy on their growth, which ends up happening fast. As a matter of fact, a plant grown hydroponically under same conditions as one grown in the soil can grow fifty percent faster.

Plus, since your plants grow faster when grown hydroponically, you get to identify defects on time and fix them right on time.

At this point, I bet you now see just how much more beneficial hydroponics gardening is, and this is just the introduction!

Is hydroponic gardening even healthy?

The nutrients supplied in a hydroponic system are not in any way different from the one in the soil; it is gotten from mineral salts. What is different in the nutrient supply is, as I mentioned, that the roots of plants grown in the soil have to go in search of nutrients; that is what makes their root systems so large. Plants grown hydroponically do not have to do this, because the nutrients go directly to the roots and in the right amount. This lets the plant spend less time growing root systems and more time growing leaves and stems. What you get as a result is strong and healthy plants.

Gradually, more commercial growers are starting to embrace hydroponic gardening over soil gardening, because it is amazing that you can control the supply of nutrients to your plants and conserve space. This ultimately boosts yield and profit.

Plants that are grown hydroponically are also not as susceptible to diseases and pests as plants grown on the soil, because of how vigorous they are. The plants possess anti-pest and anti-fungal buffers that keep them protected. This means less money spent on fertilizers, fungicides and pesticides and more safe foods, as the consumption of chemical-ridden plants no longer becomes an issue. Plants that have been sprayed with fungicides and other chemicals have detrimental effects on the health and the practice is worth doing away with.

Worthy of note is how much better hydroponic system is for the preservation of the environment. Since water circulates throughout the system, it does not get sucked into the ground or evaporate quickly. So far, hydroponics has done so much for modern day agriculture and contributed to the supply of fresh plants that are free from blemish.

This is a summary that I am sure already convinced you to consider hydroponic gardening. But just in case you are not as certain yet, we will get into the details immediately.

Why You Should Pick Hydroponic Gardening Over Soil Gardening

You Produce Chemical-Free Plants

When the soil is taken out of the equation, this translates to less pests and diseases to deal with. Plants grown hydroponically are not as susceptible to diseases and pests because of the absence of soil and how healthy they are. Pests tend to gravitate towards weaker plants and there are hardly weak plants in the hydroponic system, making pest infestations almost impossible. This in turn means that there is little or no need for fungicides and pesticides. In the end, you get plants that are not laden with toxic and unhealthy chemicals.

Saves Space

Since plants grown hydroponically rarely have bulky roots because they do not have to go in search of nutrients, you can grow more plants in smaller spaces. These plants will thrive; they have everything they need provided in the nutrient solution that is ideally measured and supplied. Planting your crops closely together rewards you with space saving.

Saves Water

So much water is saved in the hydroponic gardening system. In the traditional soil garden system, large volumes of water are expended in watering the plants, this is done so that a significant part of the water gets absorbed by the soil and sucked up by the roots of the plants. Unfortunately, this system is not such a great one because water ends up getting wasted.

How?

First off, after a good amount is poured out into the soil, only a reasonable amount gets to the root of the plant. The rest of the water either goes further down in the soil or evaporates. Whereas, in the hydroponic garden system, a recirculating nutrient reservoir is employed. Plant roots only take up some of the water at a time, the rest of the water is preserved for later. This preserved water in the reservoir is covered to ensure no evaporation occurs and water cannot seep through the bottom.

With this system, the amount of water that has gone into watering a plant in one day could be used for several weeks in the hydroponic system. So much water saving!

Location

Unlike in the soil gardening where you have to worry about location and external environment hospitability, the case is different in hydroponic gardening. As I mentioned before, everything in the hydroponic system is under your control, you are the boss. As a result, you would not have to worry a lot about location (you can't do it anywhere); first because you do not even need so much space and secondly, you can control the external environment of the plant. Since hydroponic systems do not require so much space and strategic locations, you can set up your hydroponic garden in urban areas that have little space without worrying. You can also grow your plants close to the market, thus, reducing transportation costs. As regards controlling the external environment of the plants, you are in charge of the nutrient supply and the light. There are artificial lights you can use when there is little or no access to sunlight for whatever reason. The seasons have no effect whatsoever on the hydroponically grown plants because you control the environment, not the seasons. This means you can grow a plant in a season when it is difficult to grow it, this earns you more profit.

Impressive Growth of Plants

In soil gardening, plants take so much time and energy developing root systems for searching for nutrients, water, and oxygen. As a result, they do not grow as fast because not as much time and energy is geared towards developing the leaves, stem, and most importantly, fruit.

On the other hand, plants grown hydroponically get to grow much faster because they have all of the nutrients, oxygen and water right at their roots (I would say at their fingertips if they had fingers, but you get the point). Since they do not have to do so much searching for nutrients, oxygen, and water, they can spend all their time growing. This way, they are grown in short periods, which means you get to have more growth cycles for other plants in a given time. Plus, the plants also grow bigger. As a result, you get more yields.

For emphasis, studies confirm that hydroponically grown plants tend to grow up to fifty percent faster and bigger than soil grown plants.

Control

Even though this has been said a lot in passing while explaining other points, this is a point too. In the soil gardening system, it is difficult to control a number of things, like amount of water the plants get, amount of nutrients gotten by the plants, the nutrient make-up of the soil, pests, diseases, pH, etc.

In the hydroponic system, all these factors are easily regulated so you do not have to beat your head. You call the shots over what nutrients and how much your plants get, how much water your plants get and how much is preserved, the pH of the oxygenated solution, the lighting and your plants are protected from pests and diseases.

No Weeding/Digging

This is good news for some. Unlike in the conventional gardening system with soils where you have to spend so much time on dirt, taking out weeds, building mounds and the likes, there is no such thing in hydroponics.

Since you are not dealing with soil, lots of soil issues give way, one of which is weeds. It is annoyingly time-consuming to spend ages doing this. With hydroponics, this problem is solved.

Cleanliness

No soil means there would be no problems. With soil comes all the unpleasant stuff like parasites, weeds, pests, and dirt. In the hydroponic system, you will not have to deal with this mess.

You can garden without getting yourself dirty.

Hydroponics is obviously the cleaner choice!

Cost

At first, the initial cost of hydroponics can look like a huge disadvantage. However, as time goes on, the ground pretty much levels up.

How do I mean?

It is much cheaper to set up a soil garden than a

hydroponic system. However, along the line, soil gardening starts to cost more. Money is spent on things like fertilizers, herbicides, pesticides, fungicides, and water.

Hydroponics, on the other hand costs more to set up, but most of these costs get cancelled out as a result of how effective the system is as regards water use, land or space use, little to no need for fertilizers, pesticides, herbicides and fungicides, quicker harvests, more yields and ultimately, more profit.

Little or No Diseases and Pests

As I said before, taking the soil out of the equation means that you would not have to deal with pests and diseases as much any longer. In the hydroponic system where a liquid media is used, it is almost impossible for pests to find their way to the plants and cause harm, it is also impossible to have to deal with soil-borne diseases.

Chapter – 3
HYDROPONIC VS AQUAPONICS

Aquaponics

Aquaponics is a symbiotic system for cultivating plants and fish for the good of all and all interested in the safe, natural yet unspoiled climate and soilless environment. Not only will it make your table healthy, delicious fruit and vegetables, but you can also choose to harvest your fish, an outstanding and nutritious source of protein that will complement your diet's plants. Whether you prefer fish as pets or food or a bit of both, it is up to you.

The aquaponics theory is straightforward: grow plants, fruit, and vegetables under hydroponic conditions without pesticides by growing fish instead of providing the plants with nutrients. While modern practices derive mostly from research conducted in the 1960s, the word "aquaponics" is probably as old as farming itself, which may have evolved as a result of observation of symbiotic systems in nature. Whatever its roots, industrialized farming has been practiced for thousands of years in Southeast Asian rice paddies. Fish in rice fields help nutrients for the crops to grow, and the plants help the water to keep the fish clean.

The ancient Aztecs of Mexico also developed a technique for planting crops on floating rafts in near soil conditions and have lived alongside Lake Tenochtitlan and need arable land. Nutrient-rich soil was dredged from the bottom of the lake and spread over rafts where plants grew. As the seed ripened into plants, its roots would penetrate the soil and the shoals into the lake underneath which the fish are abundant. Essentially, the Aztecs used natural resources in hand to practice large-scale aquaponics.

Hydroponics: What are you talking about hydroponics? Modern hydroponics can be traced back to Europe in the 17th century, but much earlier origins are argued for.

In this case, the hydroponic portion was the plant subsystem. Other, older examples frequently mentioned, are Babylon's "hanging" gardens, which are supposed to be fed by water from the river below the Euphrates. The hypothesis is that some systems were used to move the water to the top of the gardens, and the whole system was watered with a waterfall or trickle to supply each plant in the chain. However, according to ancient writers, the system was not smooth or "hanging" (Diodorus Siculus, Strabo, Quinto Curtius Rufus, Philosopher of Byzantium). There may have been less soil than in natural circumstances, but the descriptions make the terraces more similar to giant grazing plants over suspended plants than hydroponic systems.

Ancient Egyptian hieroglyphs seem to describe the process of plant cultivation in water, but it appears that there is not much information about what exactly this process was. Sometimes the Roman Emperor Tiberius, who used hydroponic techniques to grow cucumbers in proto-green houses, is credited with the first century. This might be an argument for early greenhouses, but it was soft? Finally, Marco Polo, an adventurer and trader of the 13th century, had returned from his journey to the Far East, believing that plants in China were developing on floating beds. It is doubtful, but it is uncertain whether it was an example of' true' hydroponics or some sort of aquaponic technology similar to that of the Aztecs. As we saw, Chinese and other far eastern cultures understood organized farming and gardening well.

All of this is told, and despite the little evidence, it would indeed be very surprising if ancient cultures had not experimented in water and on the water with growing plants; examples of unhealthy, naturally floating plants are found in nature, why did they not try it? The best evidence, however, appears to show that more successful models involve aquaponics or integrated farming principles more than likely.

Why choose Hydroponics for Aquaponics?

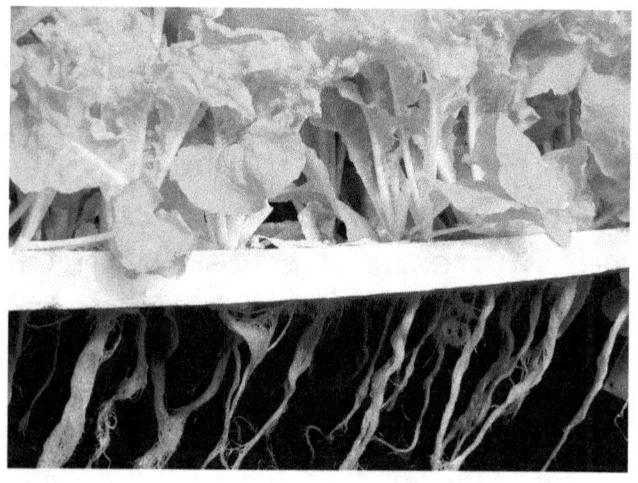

Aquaponics and hydroponics are often represented as competitive models: you choose either one, but that is a false dichotomy. In fact, aquaponics is a hydroponic farm that can be traced to ancient civilizations for hundreds, including thousands of years. It is a natural and non-chemical type of hydroponics.

Even the words used to describe them are the same: hydro is the Greek water form, aqua is its Latin version, both end with "ponic," which comes from the Greek ponos for labor or work. Nonetheless, both terms were recently invented and have different histories: the current term "aqua" panic comes from a combination of aquaculture (fish farming) and hydroponics, and hydroponics is just hydroponics. It gives the impression that the aquaponics is more recent and, in some respects, derived from the hydroponics, but as we have seen, it indicates that water pumps or integrated agriculture are actually ancestral to both modern versions. This is true of the ancient practice.

Modern hydroponics removes the natural symbiotic element from the equation and replace it with a chemical solution for the most part. This could be necessary and feasible for space exploration or in other situations where a symbiotic system is not or is not feasible, but aquaponics is the superior choice, in my opinion.

Both processes in soilless and near-soilless plants are highly successful, so why pick aquaponics? Well, the absence of chemicals enhances and improves the taste of plants grown in aquaponics, plus if you have chemical sensitivity, hydroponics cannot be for you anyway. However, fish can be used as a secondary food source if you are inclined to farm them as well. Ultimately, you grow two excellent food sources for the price of one in taking care of the fish a few minutes a day. If the fish are in good shape, the plants require little or no attention. Talk about efficiency, talk about efficiency! Some people attach themselves to fish or to vegetarians, and that is great, you are still perfect symbiosis: feeding fish, feeding fish to plants, feeding plants and filtering fish water, in an infinite, self-sustaining cycle.

You can start with a few plastic containers in your backyard or garage or convert the project into a large commercial enterprise and still have experience with a natural, hydroponic system. In no time should a simple system pay for itself. With just a few efforts to get things started, you end up with a near-self-supporting system that produces organic products of high quality without the high price of organic products. The joy you get from growing your own food is also a nice bonus. Involve the whole family and have fun. The components are relatively cheap, and you can avoid the cost of a kit or hiring professionals for you if you build it for yourself. If you are interested in gardening or would like more options about your daily diet, aquaponics is an option that you might want to take seriously.

Chapter – 4
HYDROPONIC SYSTEM (DIY)

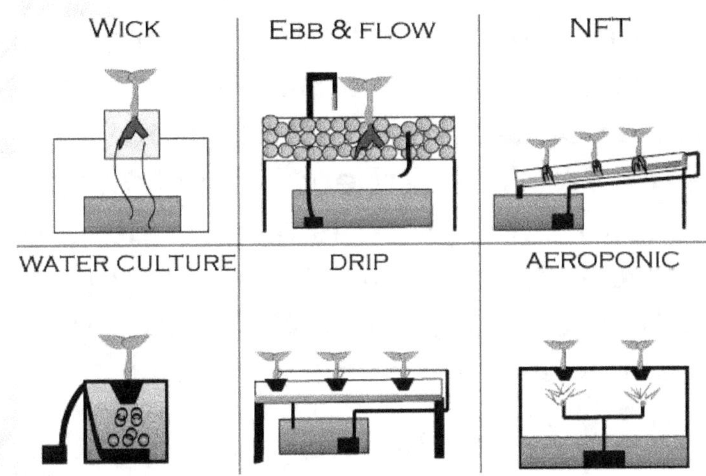

Wick System

A wick system uses a ribbon or wick made in cotton or rayon to provide nutrient solution to the origins. Normally used growth substance is vermiculite, Perlite as well as LECA.

A marijuana is encouraged within the nutrient solution in addition to a spoonful saturated in nutrient option is going to be passed via the drainage pit to the nutritional supplement tray. You need to depart 10-cm of the wick in the pot and after that ruffle the endings because of enhanced flow of nutrient payoff.

Nutrient Film Technique

This system uses an automated toaster and pump method to furnish and recycles nutrients. It is very likely to cultivate longer create using this specific system. Plants are set in an enclosed embedded 'V' form channel, though, as a result of this, plants can wither and perish as a consequence of not enough oxygen. Problems also arise if there is an electric failure or equipment failure. This technique is mainly used by lettuce manufacturers. If you are an herb enthusiast, then use NFT to nurture them you might prefer the results!

Drip System or Top Feed System

One of the principal benefits using the technique is that it may withstand momentary power/equipment collapse. Rock wool may be used while the substance. The nutrient solution is dripped about the crops alongside the remaining part of the remedy is drained back into the reservoir. The way of getting nutrient alternatives will probably be timed. It is expensive and hard to set up a trickle method. However, it is a favorite among tomato and pepper drinkers.

Aeroponics. A recent development by which crops are frozen in midair and therefore are awarded nutrition. Nutritional components are coated to the origins; their exposure to air gives them highest oxygen. In this method, the origin of nourishment and oxygen is maximized. Care has to be got to maintain up 100% relative humidity. The main disadvantage to this technique might be that the functioning of the pump and reservoir in the event of electricity failure. It is expensive to put in this procedure and can be usually used in laboratory research studies.

Dutch Bucket Method

This technique was originally used from Holland to nurture tomatoes, roses, and fauna. Including a spoonful (2.5 mills) which retains a nutrient solution at the bottom of the bucket. A pump may be used to recycle the nutrient response.

Raft Technique

In this process, Styrofoam sheets have been traditionally used to float crops fixed in baskets along with nutrient resolution. Normally, short-term crops have been cultivated for this specific system. The dilemma of stagnation is solved by dispersing air from the bottom. This technique can be used for lettuce production and to cultivate various greens.

How to Build Hydroponic System

You will want to build your own body. A number of the key advantages of making your system is you can personalize. It is similarly straightforward to assemble. Here you have got three choices to examine. Deep-water culture in this DIY manual, we will show step-by-step how to generate a simple Dry water civilization plan for 6-12 crops. This type of system is rather easy to make even for a beginner.

MATERIALS

- Air Mattress Pump + watts

- 12-inch Air rock

- air tube a couple of feet will perform

- 18-gallon bag (Rubbermaid) container with lid and this

- will probably function as a reservoir

- 6-12, 3-inch mesh pots

- Clay pellets rising medium-1.5 gallons per net pot

- Rockwool cubes

- Marker

- Box-cutter

- Power Drill with 1/2 drill piece

- Hydroponic nutrients

Guidelines

The very first thing you have to do is decide where the net baskets are becoming put. Use a marker to create some three-inch rings where the net baskets will proceed. Next is done start cutting the holes out using a box cutter.

Given that is done set aside the lid and get started washing the tote, instead utilizing 5%-10% bleach to 90%-95% water mixture.

Now drill a small 1/2-inch gap around the summit of this bag from the handle region, be certain it is close to the surface, so water won`t escape. This gap is actually the point at which the tube in the air conditioner belongs.

Presently measure a tube out of where the air conditioner will most likely be outside the machine completely throughout the hole that you just drilled into the bottom of the tote. Now slit on the region of the tubing then connect 1 finish into the air purifier tell you pit and then combine air stone into the extra finish then place air stone on bottom of the tote.

Now you can meet water. Try to meet well below in which you drilled gap, so you are ready to subtract or add water afterwards on when required. Add desired nutrition to water, follow the instructions that comprised the nutrition carefully. *optional, following place from the net baskets to the pockets in the lid, so they ought to fit fine and comfortable. Complete the net baskets using clay pellets. Next is finished place the lid on the bag and make sure the bottoms of those online strands are submerged by the nutrient solution.

I advocate first launch plants out of stone wool cubes then piled to the internet baskets filled with pellets. Nonetheless, your newcomer moderate of taste should be OK. In other words, you eventually have a completely operational Deepwater civilization.

Drip-feed method

It how you will be able to guide will describe to you precisely ways to produce a simple 4 plant trickle hydroponic program.

SUPPLIES

- 5 - 8 mill square bucket with a lid
- Small submergible Water-pump 105 GPH can do
- Air Mattress Pump
- 6-inch Air rock
- 5 ft. of 1/4 In. trickle tube
- 3"T" connectors to your trickle tube

- 3 ft. of 1/4 In. air tube

- Four 3-inch mesh pots

- 1 1/2 Pounds of clay beans hydroponic medium

- Box-cutter.

- Drill for drilling holes

- Hydroponic nutrients

Guidelines

Begin with minding four-inch diameter rings on the lid where the internet strands will move. Next to using a box cutter cut out the holes. Now drill a 3/4 in. Hole straight in the core of the lid, and then this really is to find the drip tubing. And drill a 1-inch pit close to the border of the lid that this will be suitably utilized to your own energy cable running out of the water heater and air tube coming from this air conditioner.

Next place which the water pump at the bottom of the window, then running the cable throughout the inch gap, then join 1 finish of drip tube for this. Run the tube on the surface of the inside the skillet and then across the middle hole, then cut the tube once marginally outside of your pit on the lid. Connect among these T straps to your own. Now measure and cut two portions of this tube that might run from the endings of the T connector to the middle of where the two net baskets on each side move. Place the remaining hands straps on each end. Now cut small pieces of tube for everyone these straps, so in order, they are just long enough to reach the guts of the internet pots. Now join 1 finish of air tube to the air purifier after that run the tube in the air conditioner through the inch gap and into the ground and also cut. After this end combine in the air stone and put on bottom.

Insert mesh baskets to holes and add growing medium, which could soon be clay pellets in this circumstance. Fill container utilizing water/hydroponic alternative combination. Fill-up in front of a bottom part of the internet strands is completely submerged.

Now all you have got to do would be really a plugin and add seedling to the net baskets and you are finished. I will propose starting seedlings in stone wool cubes or skillet cubes and attaching into the internet baskets using clay pellets.

Ebb and flow

An ebb and flow procedure are an easy method to make and any kind of water heater can be optional instead of compulsory, as well as are entirely unique afterward other processes, while nevertheless achieve optimum outcomes.

MATERIALS NEEDED

- Two 15 - 20-litre containers, buckets, or Rubbermaid tots
- Growing moderate: " I propose all of the clay pellets or
- even a 50/50 mixture of perlite and vermiculite
- Large sandstones or a couple of gallons of clay pellets
- 3 yards of the elastic tube, some other tube Designed for
- irrigation Can Do
- 2 tube joints
- 2 tube grommets
- Inch desk: a normally medium-sized table can perform,
- so long as It is big enough to accommodate the two
- strands

- hydroponic nutrients

- Drill to Create holes

- Silicone

Guidelines

You would like to create use of a drill and receive a hole on either side towards the bottom of those items, ensuring that the diameter will be like them inside the grommets that you're likely to probably be having to attach the joints and tube. These holes must be roughly 3-5cm on the foundation on every bucket.

Add the grommets to the pockets only made, be sure it is a tight match, when performed correctly this could be a little watertight. I advocate to use silicone round the pockets prior to incorporating the grommets to make it 100% waterproof. Let us sit is totally dry. Now combine the two joined pieces to each conclusion of the irrigation tube then add every end of the tube into the grommets of every bucket.

Now combine both the joints to every close of the irrigation tubing and then add each end into the grommets on each bucket. The 2 strands should be connecting collectively with the tube.

Currently use the dirt rocks and fill some of these ribbons just enough to cover the underside gap, which will be critical hence no perlite or vermiculite will probably clog-up in your own tube. Given that is completed put on your rising medium of taste to the exact same bucket and after that fulfill until it is about 6cm in the very notable.

Now it is possible to include your seedling in the growing moderate. After this is sometimes carried out fill out the reverse bucket of water and hydroponic nourishment to about 6cm or lower in the surface.

Now you are finished. Your bucket that you will probably be growing in should stay on the table and into flood plan put an extra bucket on the dining table will be transferred to the skillet. To empty place exactly the exact same bucket beneath the table, easy right? You need to flood your body approximate 5 times daily for 20-30 minutes in any given period and drain hence.

Chapter - 5
CHOOSING THE RIGHT SITE FOR YOUR GARDEN

Humidity

In order to maintain conditions suitable for plant growth in the system, it is necessary to provide a number of parameters, the first of which is humidity. In conditions of high humidity, the leaves of plants grow larger. Their maximum growth is observed at 60-80%. But it is better not to stick to the extreme numbers and set the humidity at 65-75%. Cuttings will need more moisture - up to 90%, and 60% is enough for seed germination.

During late flowering, it is best to use minimal humidity to avoid mold.

Humidity is a relative concept: there is much more water in hot air than in cold air. The used percentage humidity parameter is associated with water, which air is able to hold at a given temperature. This indicator is completely unrelated to the total water content in the air. At ten degrees and 100%, the relative humidity of water in the air will be half as much as at the same humidity, but at 20°C. This means that any increase in temperature in the room will lead to a decrease in humidity.

Accordingly, if the lighting turns off and the temperature drops, the humidity increases. So, darkening the room for the dark period of the cycle, it is worth running the hood for a few minutes to remove excess moisture. Otherwise, it will settle on the leaves in the form of dew and can serve as an environment in which pathogens multiply. If the lighting is on, the humidity drops, so do not immediately start the hood to keep CO2 produced at night.

If the humidity has dropped below 40%, and the air outside is too dry to raise the humidity, ventilation is indispensable: you will need a household humidifier. The air outside is usually cooler than the one in the room, therefore, once inside, it heats up and loses moisture. So even if the air outside is initially humid, it is not suitable for increasing humidity in the greenhouse.

In cold weather, it is better to cover the ventilation so that the air in the room warms up. Plants produce a lot of moisture, so it is even possible to use a dehumidifier. Plants prefer stability, so sharp changes in humidity are best avoided. If the leaves are bent up, this may be due to a rapid loss of moisture, rather than an unbalanced diet, so do not rush to add corrective substances: it may be a matter of humidity.

Ventilation

Ventilation is needed, powerful and reliable, capable of updating all the air in the room in one minute. However, if the fan is too powerful, it will be difficult to ensure constant humidity. You can use an exhaust fan that can replace the air in the room in 4-6 minutes - this is enough, and the atmosphere will be stable in the room.

It is necessary to use different types of ventilation in parallel: an exhaust fan mounted on an outlet in the wall under the ceiling - it will blow air from the room; an outlet with an air intake located on the floor, in the opposite corner to the hood of the room, while the air intake must supply air from the basement or from the north wall of the house, it will not interfere with installing a protective net from dust and insects, if this does not interfere with the passage of air; circulation fans will make the air in the room homogeneous, exclude cold or hot abnormal zones, direct them better directly to the stems, which will allow air to be removed from under the crown, making the spread of diseases and insects more difficult.

The exhaust fan is calculated simply. The volume of the room in cubic meters is multiplied by 12 (updating every five minutes - 12 times per hour). The resulting figure is an indicator of the corresponding fan. But there can be various barriers to the airflow. Thus, a carbon filter significantly reduces fan performance if air from the outside enters through the pipe, each of its elbows is an additional obstacle. Too small air intake will reduce fresh air. All these factors can be considered by taking a fan with a performance 25% higher than the calculated one.

Carbon Dioxide

The plant feeds on sunlight while consuming the carbon dioxide needed for photosynthesis, during which the carbohydrate necessary for the plant is formed and oxygen is released. This reaction is a source of energy for metabolism and, ultimately, for all life on earth, since plants are food for all life forms, including humans.

But the plant also breathes, while oxygen

is absorbed, which, when combined with a carbohydrate, releases carbon dioxide and energy. The plant breathes day and night, absorbing CO2 for photosynthesis and releasing it when breathing. As a result, more oxygen is released than carbon dioxide, although oxygen is not released at night.

Gas exchange of the plant is carried out through the pores - stomata, which are located on the underside of the leaves. In dry, hot weather, stomata close, and the plant slows down metabolism. But even when they are wide open, water vapor vaporized by the plant interferes with the absorption of CO2. In the hydroponic cultivation method, the root zone has unlimited water supply, the stomata do not close, and a good supply of carbon dioxide supports the plants in continuous growth mode.

When the first plants appeared millions of years ago, the atmosphere was much more saturated with carbon dioxide than now. Perhaps that is why the mechanism of its absorption is imperfect, and additional doses of CO2 to plants are useful. Increased carbon dioxide helps plants withstand elevated temperatures. Permanent ventilation will ensure the flow of this gas and remove excess moisture.

A piece of rather amusing advice to talk about plants has a practical basis: a person exhales quite a lot of carbon dioxide during a conversation, to which plants respond with active growth. If you want to provide the greenhouse with additional CO2, you can use sugar with yeast or vinegar with baking soda. You can buy ready-made carbon dioxide in a bottle, although the issue of regulating the amount of gas in the room is not so simple. There are sensors that measure CO2 and maintain its level automatically.

Frost-sensitive period

Frost can kill a crop or cause serious damage. To some point, severe frosts will even reach the walls of a greenhouse, destroying plants inside. Even plants that are generally frost-tolerant can be severely damaged if the frost occurs at the wrong time of the year: Virtually all fruit or floral buds are susceptible to frosting.

If frost is likely to occur at a time near the opening of flowering buds, fruit development may be stopped even if the rest of the plant is not affected. Frost consumes some young seedlings. Tender, lush young growth is more frost sensitive. You need to know when frosts are likely to occur at a particular site and select crops that do not have a high risk of frost damage for that site.

Day length

Along with temperature it is the most important factor for the formation of flower buds and for the development of fruit. For some plants, for you to achieve a good crop, the appropriate sequence of day-length must take place. For other species, there must be a minimum or maximum duration of a day before flower buds develop. For example, of flowering to occur, African violets require at least 16 hours of daylight-or artificial light.

Brightness

The quality of light is just as important for some plants as the duration of the light cycle. Where light intensities are too small, many vegetables and herbs do not achieve the same quality or yield amount. Other plants require lower light intensities and prefer shaded environments.

A location obscured by tall trees or surrounding tall buildings will have lower light intensities than one facing off the afternoon sun. A valley site may have lower luminous intensities than one on a hill or flat plain.

Rainfall

There is usually less need to cover hydroponic facilities in low to medium rainfall areas than in heavy rainfall areas, where the runoff will dilute nutrient solutions or leach nutrients out of the system.

The Optimal Temperature in Hydroponics

The temperature of the air is a very important external factor for the hydroponic plant culture site. This factor largely controls the speed of chemical reactions, enzymatic metabolism, and the development of plants (germination, a transformation of vegetative buds into reproductive buds).

The temperature that the farmer must maintain in his space of culture depends above all on the geographical origin of the cultivated plant. Indeed, these have special requirements in terms of temperature throughout their development: for germination, vegetative growth, floral induction.

It should be of note that metabolism is the set of chemical transformations that take place in cells or living organisms. These reactions can be divided into two:

1.) Catabolism - the process of degradation of molecules followed by the release of energy.

2.) Anabolism - brings together the synthesis reactions of macromolecules that demand energy consumption.

How to measure the temperature, what are the biological, chemical, physical processes depending on the temperature and then manage this climatic factor for optimal development of the plants?

To know the temperature in his space of culture, the horticulturist will use a thermometer. Originally, this instrument consists of a glass tube in which expends a quantity of mercury or colored alcohol. These instruments are simple and of sufficient accuracy for horticultural use. However, mercury thermometers can easily break down and spill the toxic metal into the culture space. With high temperatures, mercury vaporizes in the air and can be inhaled by people in the growing space.

Reminder: When an accident occurs with a thermometer, mercury must be collected in a cardboard box, put in an airtight plastic bag, and taken to a pharmacist or specialized waste treatment center. Never use a vacuum cleaner to remove mercury from a broken thermometer. (The heat will vaporize the mercury into the atmosphere, it is not eliminated, but it is transferred from the ground to the air...).

The digital thermometers are less harmful to the environment and more convenient for the farmer. The measurement of the temperature is carried out by means of a junction diode in which circulates a constant electric field. The temperature variation of the culture space varies the dynamic resistance of the dipole. The temperature is displayed directly on a screen (LCD) and most of these instruments also indicate the minima and maxima.

Some models have an external temperature sensor (probe) that allows you to know the temperature outside and inside the shelter. This is important for heating management: the greater the difference in temperature with the outside, the more it will be necessary to heat to reach the desired temperature (set point temperature).

Chapter - 6
BEST PLANT FOR HYDROPONICS GARDENING AND NUTRITION

First of all, it is necessary to know that cuttings rooted in water are ideal for starting hydroculture because, for them, it is much easier to adapt to the expanded clay substrate since it is mainly composed of water.

If you want to start with the cultivation of hydroculture plants, there is a great variety to choose from. If you are a lover of aromatic herbs, the rosemary plant is perfect for growing in hydroculture if you start from cutting; otherwise, you can choose other types of ornamental and very decorative plants, such as Ficus, Calathea, Pothos, Dracena, and Philodendron.

All plants characterized by leaves of tropical origin are well suited to hydroculture, such as the orchid and all those species that present a rapid development to the root system.

And what about flowering plants? In these cases, the most recommended species for home hydroculture are Hibiscus, Spathiphyllum, Kalanchoe, Anthurium, or Saintpaulia. Still, nothing prevents you from trying to cultivate other types of plants as well.

What about succulents? Succulents have a more complicated situation since they do not tolerate excess humidity. Therefore, the recommended species for hydroculture are aloe, succulent plants, and - as anticipated above - orchids.

Lettuce

Growing salad in hydroponics is elementary, much more than it might seem, even for those who start from scratch and approach the hydroponics world for the first time.

Once you have identified the variety of salad that best suits your needs and tastes, you must obtain the seeds that you will easily find online.

Then you will have to buy rock wool cubes (Rockwool) and net jars, a mini-green to store them in the warm, in a protected environment and with net pots, designed precisely for the needs of plants that are grown with hydroponic and aeroponic systems. Therefore, a small hydroponic or aeroponic system will be needed.

The salad seeds must be placed inside the moistened rock wool cubes (it is recommended not to insert more than five seeds for each cube) only with water and then placed inside the mini-greenhouse, at a temperature that can oscillate between 73°F (23°C) and 82°F (28°C).

One aspect to check - when using rock wool cubes - is the amount of water they absorb, because an excessive amount of liquid could cause the roots to rot and drown them. For this, it is always advisable to check the liquid levels present and possibly wring out the cubes to let out the excess water.

With the right amount of water and the ideal temperature, lettuce seeds will begin to germinate after about 48 hours. When you see the first roots appearing from the rock wool cubes (both from the sides and the base), it means that the time has come to transfer the newly born seedlings to the special mesh pots, which will first be filled with expanded clay and then settled in the hydroponic system you have chosen (or aeroponic). The seedlings inserted in the aeroponic system will then be fed with a special nutrient solution based on water and fertilizers to provide everything they need. It is vital to avoid any fertilizer during the germination phase and then start with a halved dose compared to what is recommended on the package.

Fertilizers for the cultivation of Hydroponic salad

By using suitable fertilizers and in the right dose, the roots of the lettuce seedlings are allowed to develop better and faster than they would use with a traditional cultivation system, also because - in this way - the roots can receive and assimilate nutrients faster.

To grow the seedlings in a healthy and fast way, thus strengthening their root system to make it more robust, it is possible to opt for some special fertilizers, which contain fundamental substances capable of promoting and increasing growth, accelerating absorption nutrients, and keep the most common salad diseases away. Fertilizers play a central role in the life and health of the plant. Since the hydroponic and aeroponic system does not provide for the presence of fertile soil, to ensure that the salad receives all the nutrients, it is essential to use the right fertilizers to be able to grow plants properly. Strengthening the root system of salad plants and preventing pests means growing healthy, strong, and vigorous plants capable of returning a good harvest.

Hydroponic salad: parameters to monitor

At this point, once the cultivation has started, it is appropriate to keep under control some fundamental values for the health and growth of each plant, such as the pH, which will determine the ability – by the cultivated plant – to correctly absorb the available nutrients.

In order for salad plants to absorb all nutrients correctly, the pH must be slightly acidic, and to ensure that it is always such, it is advisable to often monitor the situation with manual tests. For example, cheap and easy-to-use paper strips for pH testing can be used.

Tips and tricks for a perfect Hydroponic salad

To create a suitable and protected environment, it is recommended to repair and check the salad plants inside a grow box to make them grow well, healthily, and faster, without weighing on the cost of the bill.

Among the advantages of using the grow box, there is undoubtedly that of being able to more easily control the temperature than a larger environment and, therefore, less controlled, better manage ventilation, ensure the right lighting (thanks to the reflective mylar sheet present inside the grow box which allows the light to be effectively propagated).

But when will you get your first salad crop?

Much depends on the variety chosen and cultivated, but – in general – it is possible to say that the time required varies between 4 weeks and 80 days. By choosing different varieties and managing the aeroponic system, you can have a fresh, tasty, and healthy salad at any time of the year.

To help grow, salad plants should be adequately lit: the best solution is to use HID discharge lamps or LEDs, but a good compromise can also be found by using fluorescent lamps.

To better manage the lighting of the salad plants, it is advisable to activate the lights for 12 hours a day, thus ensuring 12 hours of darkness.

For beginners, it is advisable to purchase a simple lighting set consisting of 4 CFL lamps, sufficient for home cultivation.

Strawberries

Cross and delight of many professional and amateur growers, the strawberry is a problematic fruit, especially if grown out of season and in unsuitable environments. All difficulties are overcome, especially for those who choose the above-ground cultivation, better known as hydroponic cultivation.

The more than tested technique, especially in strawberry cultivation, offers more than exciting advantages:

- production is standardized.

- there is a considerable saving of energy and water, which is used more rationally.

- production is better in quality and quantity.

- the problem of diseases, molds, and pests that multiply on contact with the ground are entirely forgotten.

Those who choose the hydroponic technique also have the opportunity to produce strawberries in at least two different periods of the year: from October to December and throughout April and May.

If we also take into consideration that once planted, the plants begin to bear fruit after 45 days. It is well understood why this choice is shared by many growers and lovers of indoor cultivation.

Anyone who chooses to switch to this type of technique must first thoroughly wash the roots of their seedlings and insert them in a small pot that contains expanded clay or alchemy of vermiculite and perlite.

It is also essential to have a container that can hold at least 10 liters of water (for each seedling), better if impermeable to the passage of light to avoid the formation of algae and mushrooms.

Among the most popular hydroponic cultivation methods for strawberries, there is the one called NFT hydroponics: to make it simple with this system; it is possible to achieve a good circulation of all the nutrients that the roots need. Everything is automated thanks to the use of a timer that alternates between full and dry moments, essential for the roots to have the right oxygenation.

Obviously, it is essential to have the right fertilizer, which in this case, is composed of nitrogen and potassium and water with the correct pH, which should always be adjusted between 5.5 and 5.6. To make the job easier, there are active acidity regulators on the market.

Finally, you must have the right lighting, and in this case, the lamps for indoor cultivation will be a potent ally.

Once you start your strawberry cultivation, domestic or industrial, it is good to keep in mind that the plant must be regularly pruned: it is wrong not to cut excess leaves, especially before flowering. These will unnecessarily weaken the plant and could favor the creation of mushrooms that are particularly harmful to the future growth of strawberries.

Also, despite the impatience shared by many growers, it is good that the fruit is harvested only when red and ripe, better still if in times of darkness.

Tomatoes

Quality and quantity with Hydroponic tomato cultivation

Tomato is a genuinely functional vegetable in hydroponic culture. It reacts very well to the so-called "soilless cultivation," this because it can easily adapt to different types of substrate and does not require demanding agronomic management.

In tomato hydroponics, multiple substrates can be used:

• Rock wool

• Peat

• Perlite

• Coconut fiber

• Compost

And with all, you can achieve magnificent results. The only precaution that must be paid in the hydroponic cultivation of tomatoes is the temperature. Indeed, excessive maxims could affect the floral drop and, therefore, on the quantity and quality of the product.

Kitchen herbs

The new home dream is to have a thousand and one aromatic herbs on the terrace or the balcony to flavor your dishes with a personal, fresh, and eco-friendly touch. This is why hydroponics has been so successful.

The Greeks already knew it, Francis Bacon spoke about it in 1627 and today hydroponics (literally the art of growing plants in water) is well appreciated in the industrial and domestic field.

The hydroponic cultivation of aromatic herbs has five remarkable qualities:

1. the yield of the product that is developed

through indoor cultivation is better.

2. growth is faster.

3. the taste is more intense.

4. the cultivation technique is environmentally sustainable.

5. the water expenditure decreases drastically.

With hydroponic cultivation at home, it is possible to grow any aromatic plant, whether it is parsley, basil, thyme, rosemary, oregano. Still, you can also choose to grow lettuces, tomatoes, strawberries, and who knows what else.

In short, hydroponics allows at reduced costs and with a disarming simplicity to make your terrace or balcony a garden of wonders, a vertical garden, an urban oasis.

The roots of our aromatic seedlings will seek support on an inert substrate often made up of expanded clay, pralines, coconut fiber, or other similar materials. Of course, the irrigation that the plant receives must be rich in inorganic compounds that will be able to give it all the nutrients that generally come from the earth. Your cultivation of aromatic herbs will surely provide unparalleled satisfaction.

Chapter - 7
PEST CONTROL

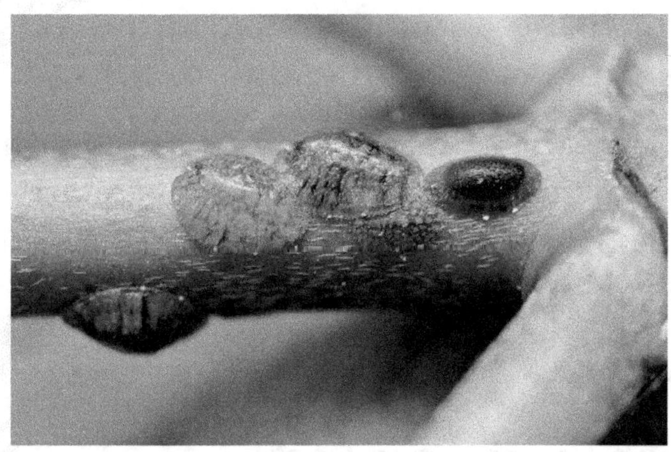

We have made it through setting up our own hydroponic garden, picking plants, learning about nutrients, and figuring out how we can maintain it. But now we have come across a whole new issue: Pests. Our setup provided a great environment for our plants to grow. But it also created an environment which pests love, and we even filled it with tons of healthy plants for them to eat. This would be fine if they provided some kind of service to our plants but all they want to do is snack on them and leave them wilted and yellowed.

We will take a look at the most common pests that hydroponic growers encounter, and we will see how you can spot them in your own garden. Our number one defense against pests is to prevent them from making our gardens their home in the first place, so we will learn some of the techniques used to detect them early and prevent an infestation.

Pests are not the only problem we face as hydroponic growers. Disease is also something we must be vigilant in spotting, identifying, and handling. To this end, we will look at some of the more common diseases and how we can prevent them.

Common Hydroponic Pests

While there are many pests that can try to make our gardens their home, there are certain pests that show up with more regularity than others. These pests fall into five key categories: spider mites, thrips, fungus gnats, whiteflies, and aphids. If you find yourself with an infestation of pests, it is a safe bet that they will fall into one of these five categories.

Spider Mites

Out of all five types of pest, spider mites are a particularly annoying one. While they are less than a millimeter long, these little guys are actually tiny spiders. Because they are so small, they tend to start damaging your plants before you even notice that they have taken up in your garden. Spider mite damage will look like tiny brown and yellow spots on the leaves of your plants. While they do not look like anything serious when there are only a couple of bites, this damage adds up quickly to really wreak havoc on your garden.

To spot a spider mite infestation, there are two key signs to look out for. While the damage on your plants can be a telltale sign, it does not specifically tell you that spider mites are the problem. To spot a spider mite infestation you should check your plants to see if you can spot any spider-like webbing. Another way to check for spider mites is to use a tissue or clean rag to gently wipe the bottoms of your leaves. If you come away with streaks of blood, this will tell you that you have a spider mite problem.

One way of handling spider mites is to wash your plants down with a hose or powerful spray bottle. The force of the water can often knock the mites off of your plant and drown them in the growing medium. Spider mites also have some natural enemies ranging from ladybugs to lacewings and you may consider adding these beneficial insects to your garden to feed on the spider mite population.

Aphids

These little guys are also known as plant lice. And just like head lice, they are not all that much fun. These tiny, soft-bodied pests are pretty much able to set up in any environment. They multiply quicker than rabbits, so you want to make sure to tackle an aphid infestation as soon as possible. These pests are typically a quarter of an inch in size and can come in green, yellow, pink, black or gray varieties.

Aphids like to feed on the juices of the plant, and you can find them chewing on stems, leaves, buds, fruits, or roots. They are particularly drawn to the newest parts of the plant. If you find that your leaves are misshapen or yellowing, checking the bottom can reveal aphids. They also leave behind a sticky substance referred to as honeydew. This sweet substance can actually attract other kinds of pests, so aphids are particularly annoying little critters. This substance can also lead to the growth of fungus, like sooty mold which can cause your branches or leaves to turn an unpleasant black color. Aphids are also able to carry viruses from one plant to another so they can help nasty pathogens to spread quicker.

Like spider mites, spraying water on the leaves can dislodge them and leave them with a hard time finding their way back to your plants. If the infestation is large, dusting your plants with flour can constipate them and help convince them it is time to move on. Wiping down your plants with a mixture of soapy water can also help to kill and drive them off.

Thrips

Like spider mites and aphids, these little guys are also tiny. Often, they are only around 5 millimeters long. It can be hard to spot these little guys, but they leave damage that is clear as day. If you start to see little metallic black specks on your leaves, you probably have some thrips snacking off your garden. Leaves that thrips attack will often turn brown and become super dry because the thrips like to suck out their juices.

Thrips are small and are either black or the color of straw. They have slender bodies and two pairs of wings. Because they are so small, they look like dark threads to the naked eye. They like to feed in large groups and will fly away if you disturb them. They stick their eggs into flowers and leaves and they only take a couple of days to hatch so a thrip infestation can feel like it just happened out of the blue.

Because thrips like to lay their eggs in plants, it is super important that you remove any dead or fallen plant matter. Make sure that you inspect your plants for thrip damage and remove any that are infested. Hosing off the plants will also help to reduce their population. Ladybugs, lacewings, and minute pirate bugs all feed on thrips and can be beneficial to your garden.

Fungus Gnats

Fungus gnats are an odd one. Adult fungus gnats have no interest in harming your garden. But their larvae enjoy chewing on the roots of your plants which slows growth and opens the plant up for infection. In extreme cases, fungus gnat larvae can actually cause the death of plants. They really like areas with a lot of moisture and a high humidity. You will likely notice adult fungus gnats before you have any issue. As adults, these gnats are about three millimeters in length and kind of look like mosquitos. They tend to be a grayish-black color with a pair of long legs and clear wings. Their larvae have shiny black heads with a whitish-transparent body.

Adults typically live for a week and in that time lay up to 300 eggs. It takes half a week for the larvae to emerge but when they do, they start a two-week diet where their main dish is the roots of your plants. When they feed on your plants, they cause them to wilt, stunt their growth and cause a yellowing of their leaves. These nasty little things can have many generations living off the same plant.

If you suspect a fungus gnat infestation than you should inspect your plants by carefully turning up the soil around their stems and look for larvae. If you check a plant and it suddenly let us loose a bunch of adult gnats, then you should dispose of that plant. They really like damp soils so make sure you are not overwatering your plants. If you have a fungus gnat problem, then letting your potting medium drain longer will help to kill off the larvae and mess up the development of fungus gnat eggs. You can also spray your plants with a combination of peppermint, cinnamon, and sesame oils. This mixture is called flying insect killer and will help to get rid of gnats.

Whiteflies

About the same size as spider mites, whiteflies look like small white moths that take up residence on your plants. They are easier to spot but because they fly away when you bother them, they can be hard to kill. Like aphids, they enjoy sucking the juices out of your plant and you see their damage as white spots and yellowing of the leaves.

They tend to lay 200-400 eggs in clusters on

the underside of the higher leaves. These eggs hatch in about a week and unattractive little nymphs come out that crawl around on your leaves before they grow wings. These crawlers will spread out from the egg and find a place to start chewing on your leaves. They will stay in that spot for the next week or so before growing into young adults which will repeat the cycle of movement-feasting.

Ladybugs and lacewings enjoy eating whiteflies and so introducing them to your garden can help to kill off whitefly populations. Hosing off plants with a strong blast of water will help in reducing their numbers as well. There are a bunch of organic pesticides on the market which you can get to deal with whiteflies. These pesticides can also work for the other pests, but pesticides should be a last resort option, one that you are careful with so as not to lead to undue stress on your plants.

Chapter - 8
HOW TO KEEP YOUR HYDROPONIC GARDEN PERFECT

Happy Plants, Happy Harvest

Maintaining Your Machines

The other important things to regularly observe and maintain are the mechanical components of your hydroponics system. You want to make sure that everything is functioning in peak condition and running efficiently. You likely have one or more motorized components, like a water pump and a bubbler. You have also likely got some grow lights, and they may need new bulbs occasionally depending on the style you are using.

The one thing to remember when you are combining running motors and water is that electricity and water do not usually make good partners. You will want to regularly check to ensure that the housings on your pumps are not cracked and that their cords are not split or frayed in any way. If you like, you can put cord protectors on them, which are available from most home improvement or contractor supply stores. Be sure to also check the cords on your grow lamps for any damage. If you find anything concerning, be sure to remedy the situation immediately or take the damaged machinery out of your system.

When you were going through your initial set-up, it was advised that you run the system for a while to familiarize yourself with the components and how they normally sound and behave. One wonderful human attribute is that we tend to know how all the things in our homes sound and can identify almost immediately when something seems 'off,' like the refrigerator making an odd clunk or the furnace making a strange noise. The same should be true for your hydroponics system. If you have become accustomed to the noise it should be making; you will know right away when it is not.

You should also have saved any owner manuals or user guides for your mechanical and electrical equipment. If something goes haywire, these manuals usually include troubleshooting guides and manufacturers' contact information to help you make a diagnosis at home or decide to find a qualified repair person or facility. The information in user guides can prove invaluable because it is specific to your make and model of equipment. Many companies also provide websites with additional information that will also be of assistance to you, and live text-based chat is also becoming a popular customer service feature.

If you have no experience with repairing your own machines, please do not run the risk of injury or property damage. You can find someone with the expertise and ask them to teach you how to do it yourself or find a trusted service provider to do the work for you. If all else fails, you can upgrade your equipment with a new model. The most important thing is to have equipment in good working order all the time.

You should also check your equipment regularly for drips, leaks, and clogs in the plumbing. You do not want to lose valuable nutrient solution to a mess on the floor, which can also cause property damage and frustration. Clogs can back up the system and burn out your pumps, which is another big concern. If possible, you should flush your system a few times a year by removing the plants for a cycle and letting the system run without roots in the way. This is so you can observe your system in much the same way you did when you first set it up. Take care of any concerns promptly, and get your plants nestled back into their homes.

Should you have a power outage, there are a few scenarios that can play out. In the first scenario, your power went off during your systems 'on' cycle, and there is some nutrient solution laying in the plumbing or the plant pool. This is not harmful if the power outage is not very lengthy. When the power is restored, the system time will either reset itself, or you should manually reset it. It may be best, depending on how long the outage was, to run the pump long enough to drain the system and restart it the next day.

If your power went out during the 'off' cycle, you would have a similar problem, but in reverse. Just as you do not want your plants sitting in their solution for too long, you also do not want them to go too long without, either. If the outage is short, it should not be much of an issue. You can just give the roots a nutrient bath when the power comes back on and reset your timers for the next day. After either situation, you will just want to double-check your equipment to make sure there was no damage from an electrical surge.

In the case of a lengthy power outage, you may need to take additional steps to ensure that your plants will not be without their requirements for too long. If you have a generator, you may want to make sure your system is hooked into it, but again, check your equipment for damage from surges. If you do not have a generator or access to a generator, you will want to find a way to manually care for your plants during your extended outage. Another option might be a battery-operated pump that you can use in place of your corded pump. Because light may be an issue, you will want to open up blinds and shades to allow your plants to get as much natural light as possible and come to terms with the possibility that your plants may be a little stunted.

Chapter - 9
GARDENING SECRETS, TIPS AND TRICKS TO MAKE THE HYDROPONIC SYSTEM WORK EFFICIENTLY

Gardening is a field that has developed gradually since the start of time. Since the early days until now, people have tried to develop better techniques to deliver a more effective and easy gardening technique. Different forms and new and better strategies have evolved over the years. Another such method is hydroponics.

Hydroponics helps you to cultivate your plants

without any natural hazards throughout the year. Conventional gardening techniques require a number of external factors uncontrollable for plant cultivation.

Incontrollable variables such as different seasons, weather etc. play a key role in yield. Nevertheless, approaches that use water solution instead of soil minimize the risk associated with these variables.

These hydroponic systems can be made in your own home if you are an experienced plant gardener. You can also go online for the kits made available by the company. Such kits are available in different sizes and can be chosen according to your particular needs.

Such kits include the necessary equipment and elements such as lamps, pumps, containers, nutrient systems, etc. In any case, you will need an in-depth understanding of plants and their different aspects.

There are many different aspects that make the Hydroponics device cycle a success. Lighting is such an important aspect. It is necessary that you give the plants sufficient light to grow.

At least a good eight hours of sunlight should be given to young plants for efficient growth. Always remember that too much is bad. Make sure that light is not too high, especially when using multiple lights.

Other very important factors in hydroponics are humidity and temperature. Each living organism has an ideal level of different environmental conditions, such as humidity, temperature, etc. If plants are grown indoors, it is very important for plants to survive in a good environment.

More carbon dioxide can also be introduced into the plant for better growth. In addition to external conditions, nutrition is equally important. You will be able to better understand their nutritional needs by studying the plants you want to produce.

When you have the necessary nutrient solution in Hydroponics, you must focus on the absorption rate. This ensures that the plant can absorb nutrients without any problems to the best of its ability. The aim of a controlled environment is to be able to change every factor in growing plants to maximize their efficiency.

Air pumps and sleeves can help to improve air circulation throughout the solution. For a fact, the water used in the process can also be used over and over again. Whilst it is best to practice gardening before using the hydroponics, beginners can also grow their favorite plants and vegetables in a smaller size.

Hydroponic gardening is nothing other than soil-free planting. It is an economical way to supply plants with food and water. The soil's purpose is to provide plants with nutrients and to protect the roots of plants.

A plant uses food and water in the soil. The plant is supplied with a full nutrient solution and a growing medium in the hydroponic gardening to sustain the root plants.

It allows plants to access water and food more quickly. If you start your first hydroponic garden, a lot of resources and information can be found online. A good way to begin a hydroponic garden is to obey useful factors during gardening.

Some of them are listed below: Grow: you can grow hydroponically vegetables, flowers, and medicinal plants. Many of them include tomatoes, peppers, cucumbers, orchids, and medicinal plants. You can start a garden by buying seeds online or just buy it from garden centres.

System or method: There are six types of hydroponic systems that you can use for your greenhouse, including Ebb and Flow, Drip, Aeroponic, N.F.T and Wick System. Any device, lighting, and growing medium that suits your plants, garden size and budget can be selected.

Garden area: whether you need a small or large

hydroponic garden, you have to decide. The flow of air and the ability to control moisture and temperature in the room depending on your area of cultivation.

Your garden always needs clean water and safe electricity. A continuous water supply with a good pH level is very critical. You need the electric power supply for indoor gardening to operate water pumps, grow systems and fans.

Accessories: Depending on the complexity and size of your hydroponic garden, various accessories including light timers, fans, water pumps and meters for temperature and humidity measurement are required. Many hydroponic gardeners will help you to pick different garden needs.

Lighting system: Light is the key component if you plan to start an indoor garden. Understand your growing space and choose the perfect lighting for your garden. You can choose high intensity growing lights that provide sunshine to your indoor garden.

Nutrients: You do not use soil in hydroponic gardening to grow plants. You must, therefore, provide the plants with full balanced nutrition. Plants require six types of micronutrients, Nitrogen, Phosphorus, Potassium, Calcium, Sulfur, Magnesium, in particular.

A plant needs some small traces of vitamins, iron, boron, zinc, manganese, cobalt, and copper. Choose a perfect solution to provide sufficient macro and micronutrients for your plants.

Growing medium: hydroponic means soilless gardening and therefore soil needs to be replaced by a perfect medium of production. This rising medium provides the plants with nutrients. There are enormous varieties of growing medium that cocoa, organic soil, mats, crushed stones, and rock wool can be used.

Hydroponics is not a difficult planting strategy. In this process, the plant nutrients are liquefied during the water. A rising medium substitutes the soil for oxygen, water, and nutrients to the roots.

The first step in hydroponics is to buy your supplies. The seeds can be put in rock wool starter cubes that fit well into the typical nursery tray. The rock wool should be soaked overnight in a conditioning solution.

Place a seed in each cube.

In each cube. Place the tile under a fluorescent lamp with a semi-circular rim. Wait for the germination of the seeds and for the roots to come out of the cube base. This is the moment when the roots are transplanted into the hydroponic system.

- A large yellow pail is required to serve as the external storage that contains the food and water for your plant. The plant actually sits in a small green pail with small pants. More products include the fluorescent light bulb, root help marbles and plant food.

- Punch small holes in the smallholder to prevent too much water from flooding the roots.

- Wash the ground from the roots until you see the root system's main part. Handle the roots with great care.

- Place some marbles at the bottom of the little bowl. This can be from 1/2 inch to 1 inch to provide enough water and air for proper growth.

- Enable the roots to settle at the base to access more water. Fill the bowl with more marbles once this is finished. Inside the larger container, position the small pot until it gets balanced.

- You can illuminate the plant to speed up production. Water and feed the plant-based on hydroponic gardening standards. Nutrient, salt, and water measure. You need one Miracle Grow tablespoon, another salt tablespoon and one gallon of water.

- Combine the solution and pour tenderly on the root until the waterline is almost one inch above the bottom of the small pot in the large container.

- Make it a point for your plant to maintain. If the plant leaves turn into another color, a problem can occur. The water should also not be too low or too high. The PH balance is better known. To address this problem, change the water regularly. In any hydroponic supply store, PH level test tools can be purchased.

Chapter - 10
MYTHS AND MISTAKES

Myths

Hydroponics is a New Technology

This is a very common myth that is very popular amongst the traditionalists among us. However, as said earlier, it is just a myth. Hydroponic gardening is a very old and ancient field. It is believed that the pharaohs of Egypt loved fruits and vegetables that were grown hydroponically. Even the famous wonder of the Ancient World, The Hanging Gardens of Babylon, were supposed to be hydroponic gardens. In India, plants are grown directly in a coconut husk, hydro at the most grassroots level. It is thus proven that hydroponic gardening is not at all a new technique but an old and ancient science of cultivation.

Hydroponics is Artificial or Unnatural

Once again, this myth is highly popular amongst the traditional thinkers. Such people think that growing plants in water is against nature and is artificial. This is absolute rubbish. The growth of plants is a real and naturally occurring thing and cannot be done artificially. Plants need certain things to grow and thrive and they normally take these things from the soil. In hydroponics, we just replace the soil with water. Plants still can absorb whatever they need from the water and grow well. Unless you consider water unnatural, then you simply cannot consider hydroponic gardening unnatural.

Hydroponic gardening does not involve any kind of genetic mutation or introduction of any unwarranted and mysterious chemicals. This is not a steroid inducing system but is a perfectly natural and safe method of growing crops.

Hydroponics Harms the Environment

This is a ridiculous myth. Hydroponic gardening does not harm the environment at all. In fact, it helps the environment. Water is one of our most precious resources and because of hydroponic gardening, around 70 to 90 % of water can be saved as compared to the conventional form of gardening. Hydroponic gardening also does not have any fertilizer runoff. This runoff can pollute the soil and rivers, lakes, etc.

Hydroponics is Very Complicated and Cannot Be Done at Home Unless You Are Exceptionally Talented

Hydroponics is a very easy system of gardening that can be done by almost anyone with a love of plants. An inexpensive hydroponic system can be constructed with simple things such as a bucket, hydroponic growing medium, and hydroponic nutrients. You can definitely use advanced technology and science to create an exceptionally sophisticated hydroponic garden to produce high amounts of yield but you can also use simple, cheap, yet effective instruments and equipment if you want to do hydroponic gardening just as a hobby. As said earlier anyone can pick up hydroponic gardening, anyone means people of all ages.

Hydroponics is Far too Expensive

You can definitely use expensive and advanced technology and science to create an exceptionally sophisticated hydroponic garden to produce high amounts of yield but you can also use simple, cheap, yet effective instruments and equipment if you want to do hydroponic gardening just as a hobby. You can work on a limited budget yet produce excellent and fantastic results with ease if you are dedicated to your garden.

Not Widespread and Limited to Developed Nations

This is a rather bizarre and ridiculous myth. Hydroponic gardening is done in every corner of the world.

People do hydroponic gardening in places where the climate is unsuitable for the growth of plants or in nations where the quality of soil is not suitable for a good yield. It is also commonly used in developed and developing nations such as the USA where the soil has been abused and is no longer cultivable. In British Columbia, 90% of all the greenhouse industry is now based upon the hydroponic gardening system.

Hydroponics Must Be Done Indoors

Hydroponics is generally cultivated indoors because people have no place to cultivate plants outside but relax. You can easily grow a hydroponic garden outdoors as well. A benefit of constructing a hydroponic garden indoors is the fact that you can control the lights. Outdoors you need to depend on the sun for the light. It not impossible or hard to do hydroponic gardening outdoors. It is even possible to do soil gardening inside the house if you know how to do it.

Hydroponics Do not Need Pesticides

Well this myth is very common but unfortunately false. You do need pesticides for a hydroponic garden, but the soil-born pests are eliminated naturally because of there being no soil. There are other kinds of pests that you need to protect your plants from. You should ideally only use pesticides when you feel that your plants are under attack. To avoid the attack of pests, keep a close eye on your system. Never enter the dark room when you are unclean or have come from outdoors especially from a garden or a park.

Hydroponics Produce Huge Plants

This myth is slightly true. Every seed like every other living thing has a genetic code that has all the coding that determines the size, weight, yield, etc. of the plant that the seed will produce. Hydroponics is a well-developed system, but it is not a magical system that can force a seed of cherry tomato to grow a beefsteak tomato plant. Yes, it can help you to grow the best cherry tomatoes with the seed though.

It is quite hard to grow a seed to its highest point in soil as the makeup of the soil varies from place to place. Although the components of the soil can be controlled and manipulated, you cannot have 100% control over them. However, in the case of hydroponic gardening you have total control and freedom on the components.

You can easily manipulate them, so as to grow the best plants easily. Hydroponic gardening also consumes a lesser amount of energy as compared to soil gardening. This reserved energy is used by the plants to produce more and more yield. The plants become healthy, their foliage is dense and their flower and fruits delightful.

Hydroponics Is Used Primarily for Illegal Purposes

This myth, unfortunately, has some truth in it. However, like every other thing in this world, you can use hydroponics for a good purpose as well as a bad purpose. Sugar is a very tasty and sweet product but if used wrongly, it can give you diabetes. Similarly, dynamite is a very useful product but if used in an improper way, it can be dangerous. Hydroponic gardening is no different. Often, law enforcement officials talk about hydroponic gardening when talking about marijuana and such illegal substances. Many people thus form a relationship or connection between two things and start believing that hydroponics is exclusively used to grow illegal substances. Yes, it is true that people do use hydroponic systems for illegal purposes, but people use cars for illegal purposes too. If you cannot stop using cars, you should not stop using hydroponic gardening as an alternative kind of gardening. Remember, any power is good only until it is in safe hands. Power itself is not corrupt. The people who use it are corrupt. Likewise, hydroponic gardening is not wrong or illegal. The corrupt people who use it for their illegal benefits are wrong.

Mistakes

Since you are just now getting into hydroponics gardening, you may want to take things as slowly and as carefully as you could. One mistake could send the entire project rolling down the hill, and no one wants that. What an investment you have made, and how sad it would be to see it all amount to nothing! What you do to prevent this is to get first, a clear understanding of what your intended plants expect of you and how to attend to each of their needs.

While knowing what to do is important, you should also beware of what not to do, because doing so would mess up your project.

#1: Going Cheap by Sourcing Ineffective or Not Buying Enough Lighting

One of the most critical investments you ought to make as a hydroponic farmer is to seek the best lighting for your crops. This requires you to conduct first, substantial research in the market, and among seasoned hydroponic farmers, on the right kind of lighting, bearing in mind that different bulbs will produce different kinds of energy and light spectrums.

Also, don't expect that placing your plants next to a window is enough substitution for grow lights because usually, the light that gets in through the window is not sufficient, or strong enough to support the vigorous growth common among hydroponic plants.

#2: Designing Unusable or Difficult-To-Use Hydroponic Farms

Some beginners make the mistake of designing an unusable farm because they lack experience or because they have not dealt with hydroponics before, at least not on a large scale.

Due to inexperience, they fail to think about factors like efficiency and workflow, which leads to farms that make regular maintenance operations difficult, make harvesting difficult and do not use the space available efficiently. These inefficient gardens may also demand lots of tending, transplanting due to death of the plants, and difficulties controlling pests. Farmers also have a difficult time accessing various parts of the systems.

Now that labor is the most expensive variable cost in a farm, it is of great importance that the farms have labor-efficient designs.

The solution to this mistake is to take some considerable time to plan out and think about how the system will work, and from there, you can now build individual components. Consider all the variables, including water, nutrients, light, pests, convenience, access, redundancy, and automation, right from the start, and only start planning out the design once you have figured out each of the variables mentioned.

It would help if you went benchmarking, by visiting and talking to seasoned growers to see the systems they are operating. Go ahead and ask questions, including seeking answers to the question of what they would do differently were they to turn back and begin afresh.

Chapter - 11
BUSINESS TIPS AND INFORMATION ABOUT HYDROPONICS

Market Overview

The stats and figures for last year were quite astonishing because the Global industry of hydroponics was valued at around 23.94 billion USD in 2018. And it is now expected to touch the 6.8 compound annual growth rate by 2024. Now, in terms of the largest market of hydroponics, then European countries are ruling their hegemony here. They have approximately around 47 percent of the overall industry or global market.

There is no doubt that hydroponics is the

most prominent way of saving water and also an environment-friendly technology with a profitable business. Perhaps, that is why it has been widely promoted by the government and non-government organizations in the various parts of the world. And in terms of the drawback then maybe it is the high cost of the system. But numerous researches and experts are arduously working on this aspect too.

Scope of hydroponics

The process of hydroponic is way more straightforward than we have speculated. It involves the work of growing plants through water, nutrients solution in gravel, sand, without using the land or soil. Today, we have been watching the blast in population growth. Countries like China and India having a population of over a billion. And because of that, the food problem is growing day by day. Thousands of people are dying every day due to the lack of food.

The soils and land are shrinking day by day due to the development model of the world. So, in that case, the process or concept of hydroponic means growing without soil can be the perfect solution for the soil and the food problem.

Market Trends

Today we have been watching the boom of population. And the worst part is that 20 thousand people are adding on the list every day. Due to that, the demand for food and Security is increasing. And a continuous supply of food and significant resources to the increasing population has become a significant global threat.

The states acquire a huge part of farming land or soils on the name of development. And on the other hand, unwanted things like pests and plant diseases are creating the mess about 10 to 16 percent annually and making the condition terrible to worse.

To control the situation and for attaining sufficiency in food, the concept of hydroponic farming is the best for us. We do not know what will happen in the coming future, but right now it is the best answer for all our questions. Soilless growing technology is a space-friendly and can be done for the landless rural and urban people.

In the contemporary scenario, hydroponic technology is successfully tested on various vegetables and has the high potential to provide essential help in areas like the Middle East, where millions and billions of dollars are given to the other countries, to import the corps.

Tips for starting a hydroponic business

These are the business trends and current scenario of the hydroponic industry. And let us figure out some tips for starting a hydroponic system

1) Planning- set a blueprint

It does not matter whether you want to start a restaurant or import and export business. First of all, you need to prepare your blueprint or planning to make your business a successful one. Planning is the primary step for every work because, without planning, you cannot be able to execute your actions well.

So, let us figure out how much you want to spend on the hydroponic business and the overall.

How many systems you want to establish, types of systems, area of business, and many more things that can help you in the future!

2) Legalize your firm or business entity

It is one of the most crucial aspects of any firm. If you want to start a business, then legalize it first so that one cannot be able to steal your ideas or brand name. And off course, if it will happen, then you will have the authority to sue them or pull that person in the courtroom for their sin.

On the other hand, legalization of the firm also generates credibility and faith in the market about the brand name. Because everyone wants to work with a credible and legal company and love to share their capital with them.

3) Taxation- make provisions

Another essential that needs to be taken is that if you want to start a hydroponic business. And if you have the legal business firm, then you must have provisions for the taxation for your respective firm.

Taxation provisions will immensely help you when you sit on a chair at the end of the financial year to count down the sheet of loss and profit. And on the other hand, taxation provisions will help you to be transparent with the governmental bodies of taxation.

4) Start- business account

It is imperative to have a separate bank account for your business firm if you are running a business entity. The different bank account will help you to make your business transactions transparent from your personal account and assist in auditing work.

We have seen many cases, and most of them have now become a great example that suggests a business owner must open a separate bank account for the business. On the other hand, it will help you to get away from many obstacles of taxation authorities.

5) Prepare your all licenses and permits in order

Hydroponic business is still new in the business world despite gaining so much popularity and capital value. And it is also related to the farming and growing that refers solely to the health of people that it requires some special permits and licenses from the governmental and non-governmental bodies.

And on the other hand, it would be better for you if you have all the legal permissions and licenses because these are the biggest reasons for facing great trouble shortly. And this can lead to permanent shut down of your business.

6) Get Insured

To get insured is one of the most important yet mainly ignored aspects of the company or firm. Insurance is not only useful for any business firm but also equally important for the owner too. Because no one knows what will happen next. And to take precautions for the future is the greatest thing one can ever do.

You cannot be sure enough about your business or your future possibilities because any misshaping in the future can lead to shutting down for your firm. So, you must get insured for any financial lows, any incident or accident, disruption, temporary pause, worker's compensation, and many more.

7) Go Digital

Digital platforms are the most significant way of promoting, branding, advertising, and selling your business. Today, if you want to survive from the heinous competition, then you need to mark your presence at the digital media such as Facebook, YouTube, Instagram, and many others.

Hydroponic business is relatively new in comparison to other pre-established companies. That is why you need to promote it well, to increase the growth as well as the sales. And now social media has become the best way to find out your potential clients because every single firm and business houses are now on social media.

Why is hydroponic business getting popularity?

1) Convenient

Indeed, you have the right equipment such as hydroponic system, lights, growing medium, nutrient solutions, cloning trays, then it would be quite an easy and convenient process for you. Though there are some aspects which seem pretty arduous, if you have little knowledge and experience about it, then it would be a great learning process for you.

2) Trendy

Yes, it is one of the most popular businesses right now in the world. The hydroponic market generated a value of 23.94 billion USD last year. So, now you can imagine how immensely popular this business industry is. On the other hand, it is effortless to do because people who did not have any clue about the farming industry are now doing research and study on this method.

3) Efficient

The world is facing a significant threat of food inefficiency at the moment. Most of the lands are now listed on the name of dream development model, and the rest are facing the condition of inability to produce.

So, in the contemporary time, the concept of hydroponic farming is the best solution for the threat of food and farming inefficiency. Through this, we can produce crops and vegetables with the massive growth rate. And also earn some great profit. With the right use of the nutrient solution, lights, appropriate water, and temperature, we can expedite the growth.

So, these are essential business tips for those who want to start a hydroponic system. There are many reasons why the hydroponic method is gaining immense popularity and marching towards the biggest solution of inefficiency. So, if you want to start a business, they must consider these points.

Conclusion

Starting with a definition of hydroponics, we have covered a lot of information that will help you to get started on your own hydroponic garden. Before we close, let us go over a brief summary of what we covered and share some words on where to go from here.

Hydroponics has been around for literally ages, but it is only just starting to pick up some serious interest. These gardens can take a bit of work to set up and maintain but they offer a great way of growing crops. We focused here on those looking to get started with hydroponics, so we tailored our information towards the beginner. The lessons we covered, however, have everything the beginner needs to get started and begin the road to expert.

We have six primary setups to choose from when it comes to what kind of system we want to set up. We saw how to set up deep water, wicking and drip systems. These are the easiest systems for DIY setups and beginners but there are also aeroponics, ebb and flow and nutrient film technique systems. These systems are more complicated than is recommended for a beginner one, but I encourage you to research these more as you get more comfortable with hydroponics.

There are four key elements that we looked at as the operation cycle of the hydroponic garden. These are soiling, seeding, lighting, and trimming. By understanding how each of these elements works, we are able to handle the growing cycle of our plants. There are many options available for soiling and several for lighting. Finding the combination that is right for you will take some research, but it should ultimately be decided on what plants you want to grow.

Speaking of plants, we have seen that there are a ton of plants that work really well in hydroponic gardens. Herbs grown in a hydroponic garden have 30% more aromatic oils than those grown in soil. Lettuce in particular absolutely adores growing hydroponically. Each plant has its own preferences when it comes to how much water it wants, the pH level it likes best and the temperature that it needs to grow. For this reason, we have to research our plants and make sure that we only grow those that are compatible together.

We also learned how to mix our own nutrient solutions so that we can provide our plants with what they need to grow. There are a lot of pre-mixed options available for purchase as well. Taking control of our own mix is just another way we are able to get closer to our plants and provide for them to the best of our ability.

The importance of maintaining a clean garden cannot be stressed enough and so we spent time learning how we care for our gardens. To do this, look at how often each step of maintenance needs to be performed and plan ahead so that you do not forget. It is super important that we take care of our plants because we do not want them in dirty environments, nor do we want them to be overly stressed. A dirty environment and a stressed plant are a recipe for infestation and infection.

We explored some of the most common pests that attack our plants. However, we did not cover all of them. That would take a whole book. The pests we covered are the most likely ones you will have to deal with but that does not mean they will be the only ones. It is a good thing we also learned how to prevent pests. The preventive steps we learned will also help us to spot any pests we did not cover. If you find something you do not recognize in one of your traps, then you know it is time for more research. Remember too that not every insect is a pest, some help us out by eating pests!

Infection is a risk with all gardens and so our number one tool in preventing harmful pathogens from attacking our plants is to make sure that our plants are nice and strong. We clean our gardens, we provide them with nutrients mixed to their liking, we give them the love and care they need and in doing this we keep them healthy and unstressed. While infection can still take hold in a healthy plant, it is far more likely to attack stressed plants.

Finally, we looked at mistakes that are common to beginning hydroponic gardeners. We also exploded those myths that surround hydroponics to dispel the lies and untruths surrounding our newfound hobby. Searching online for tips or mistakes will reveal many discussions with hydroponic gardeners that are written specifically to help beginners like you to have the easiest, most enjoyable time possible getting into this form of gardening.

If you are excited to get started, then I suggest you begin planning out your garden now. You will need to dedicate a space for it and pick which system is most appealing to you and your skill level. Write down the plants you are most interested in growing and begin gathering information about them; what environment do they like best? What temperature? How much light do they need? What pH level?

Once you know what plants you want to grow and what system you want, you can start to build a shopping list. Along with the hardware to set up the system itself, do not forget to get some pH testing kits and an EC meter. Also make sure you have cleaning material, as you know now how important it is to sanitize and sterilize your equipment. This is also a great time to build your maintenance schedule.

The information that we covered will take you from beginner and, along with the application of practice, turn you into a pro in no time. But most importantly, do not forget to have fun!